iMath Readers

The Science Olympiad:
Proportions and Ratios

by Renata Brunner-Jass

Content Consultant
David T. Hughes
Mathematics Curriculum Specialist

NORWOOD HOUSE PRESS
Chicago, IL

Norwood House Press
PO Box 316598
Chicago, IL 60631

For information regarding Norwood House Press, please visit our website at
www.norwoodhousepress.com or call 866-565-2900.

Special thanks to: Heidi Doyle
Production Management: Six Red Marbles
Editors: Linda Bullock and Kendra Muntz
Manufactured in the United States of America in Brainerd, Minnesota. 231R—052013

Library of Congress Cataloging–in-Publication Data

Brunner-Jass, Renata.

The science olympiad: proportions and ratios/by Renata Brunner-Jass; content
consultant, David Hughes.
p. cm.—(iMath)

Includes bibliographical references and index.

Summary: "The mathematical concepts of proportions, ratios, and scaling are
introduced as students partake in the regional Science Olympiad. Additional
concepts include scale factors, unit rates, and tape diagrams. This book also
features a discover activity, a connection to history, and mathematical and
scientific vocabulary introductions"—Provided by publisher.

Audience: Age 10–12
Audience: Grade 4 to 6

ISBN 978-1-59953-576-0 (library edition: alk. paper)
ISBN 978-1-60357-545-4 (ebook)

1. Ratio and proportion—Juvenile literature. I. Title.

QA117.B779 2012
513.2′4—dc23
2012036813

CONTENTS

Note to Caregivers:

Throughout this book, many questions are posed to the reader. Some are open-ended and ask what the reader thinks. Discuss these questions with your child and guide him or her in thinking through the possible answers and outcomes. There are also questions posed which have a specific answer. Encourage your child to read through the text to determine the correct answer. Most importantly, encourage answers grounded in reality while also allowing imaginations to soar. Information to help support you as you share the book with your child is provided in the back in the **Additional Notes** section.

Bold words are defined in the glossary in the back of the book.

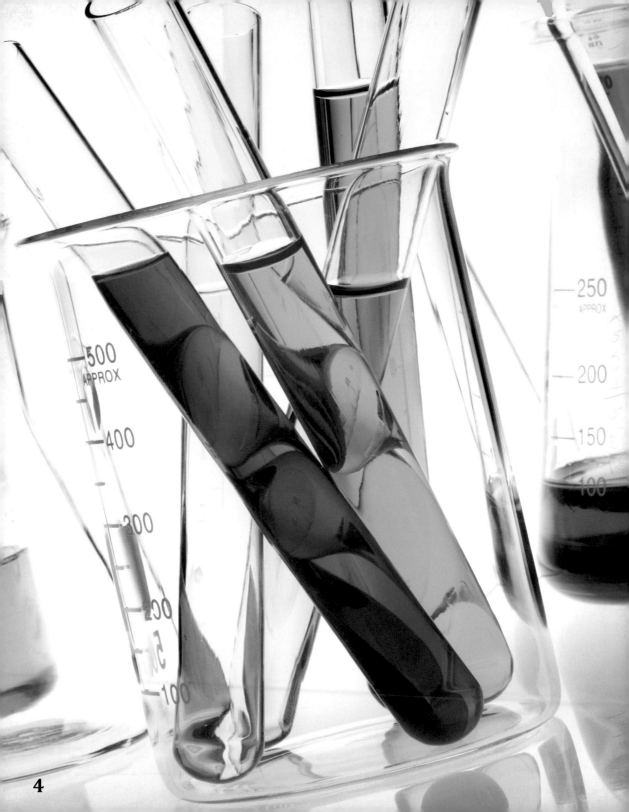

4

Getting Ready

Mr. Mead leads our science club. We spend much of the school year participating in a variety of science activities. These activities help prepare us for the Science Olympiad. They focus on five main areas of interest. These are earth and space science, biology, chemistry, physics, and engineering.

There are two main types of events at a Science Olympiad. There are "mystery events" that remain unknown until the day of the Olympiad. That is, students don't know what tasks to expect. There are also "work-at-school" events. For these, students plan and build or grow things ahead of time. Then, they take their projects to the Olympiad.

Both mystery events and work-at-school events may require students to use models. Models are descriptions, drawings, mathematical explanations, or copies of objects or events. Students use words, numbers, pictures, computer skills, and materials to create models.

Our school is a K–8 school. So, at this year's Science Olympiad, we had one K–2 team, one 3–4 team, and one 5–8 team. It was an exciting, action-packed science experience for everyone.

How Do They Compare?

Proportions are important in many models students make for the Science Olympiad. A proportion is a mathematical statement. It shows that two **ratios** are **equivalent**, or the same.

Ratios compare numbers and are written in one of three ways. Think about the relationship between cats and the number of legs belonging to those cats. If there's one cat, the ratio is 1 to 4, or 1:4, or $\frac{1}{4}$. If there are two cats, the ratio is 2 to 8, or 2:8, or $\frac{2}{8}$.

$$\frac{1}{4} \times \frac{2}{2} = \frac{2}{8}$$

The proportion may be written: 1:4 = 2:8. No matter how many cats there are, the relationship between number of cats and number of legs is always the same. So, 1:4 is equivalent to 2:8, 3:12, and 4:16.

Idea 1: We can use a **tape diagram** to solve a problem involving a proportion. Say that a painter wants purple paint. Liters of blue and red paint are mixed in a ratio of 3 to 2 to make purple. How many liters of blue and red paint are needed to make 65 liters of purple paint?

3 units of blue paint + 2 units of red paint = 5 units of purple paint

3 to 2, or 3:2

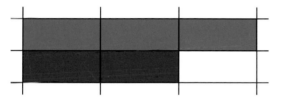

5 parts $\longrightarrow$ 65 liters
1 part $\longrightarrow$ 65 ÷ 5 = 13 liters
3 parts $\longrightarrow$ 3 × 13 = 39 liters
2 parts $\longrightarrow$ 2 × 13 = 26 liters

The painter needs 65 liters of purple paint. It takes 5 parts of blue and red paint to make one liter of purple paint.

The painter needs 39 liters of blue paint and 26 liters of red paint to make 65 liters of purple paint. Do you think using a tape diagram to find the missing term of a proportion is useful? Why or why not?

Idea 2: We can create a **table** to solve a problem involving a proportion. The parts of a proportion are called its **terms**. If we know three of the terms, we can find the fourth. For example, say a team wants to make several models of atoms, or the smallest units of matter. They plan to use foam balls. If four foam balls cost 5 dollars ($5.00), how much do 24 foam balls cost? Look at this problem as a proportion:

$$\frac{4 \text{ foam balls}}{5 \text{ dollars}} = \frac{24 \text{ foam balls}}{? \text{ dollars}}$$

Number of Foam Balls	4	8	12	16	20	24
Cost ($)	5	10	15	20	25	30

The total price of 24 foam balls is 30 dollars ($30.00). Do you think using a table of equivalent ratios is useful for finding the missing term of a proportion? Why or why not?

Idea 3: We can find a **unit rate** to find the fourth term in a proportion. Say a teacher needs to buy 15 water-testing kits for a class to use in a field activity. Two kits sell for $5.00.

The following ratio represents the cost of the kits:

$$\frac{2 \text{ kits}}{5 \text{ dollars}} \text{ or } \frac{2}{5}$$

Next, write a proportion to represent the problem.

$$\frac{2 \text{ kits}}{5 \text{ dollars}} = \frac{15 \text{ kits}}{? \text{ dollars}}$$

Find the price of one kit.

$$\frac{2}{5} \div 1 = \frac{2}{5} \div \frac{2}{2} = \frac{1}{2.50}$$

One kit costs $2.50. Multiply this cost by the total number of kits.

The following diagram combines the steps for using a unit price to solve a proportion.

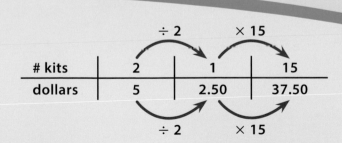

The total cost of 15 kits, based on a unit price, is $37.50. Do you think finding a unit rate to find the missing term of a proportion is useful? Why or why not?

Smooth "Scaling"

A **scale** is a ratio that compares lengths. It compares the length of an object in a drawing, map, or model to the object's length in the real world. For example, imagine a map of a valley drawn to a certain scale. The length and width of the valley on the map are proportional to the length and width of the real valley.

Trace or draw a **polygon**, or closed shape with three or more sides. Measure each side. Use a protractor to measure each angle. Write the measurements on the drawing.

Next, draw a **similar** polygon. That is, draw a polygon that has the same shape but is a different size. To do this, keep all of the angle measures the same, but multiply the length of each side by the same number.

For example, look at the four-sided polygons below. Polygons with four sides are called **quadrilaterals**. The quadrilaterals below are similar. Their **corresponding** angles have equal measures. That means that the angles in the same position in both quadrilaterals have the same measure. And, the lengths of each shape's sides are proportional. So, for example, the ratio of the length of side A to the length of side B is proportional to the ratio of the length of side E to the length of side F.

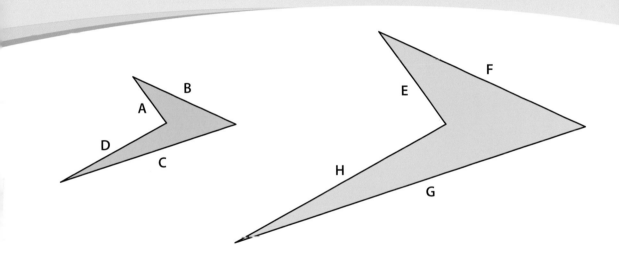

How could you use ratios to help you find other similar polygons?

Will you:
• use a tape diagram?
• use a table of equivalent ratios?
• use a two-step method for calculating a missing term?

Currents and Explosions

Sometimes, the older students in the Science Club help the younger ones. And other teachers help Mr. Mead.

Ms. Nash, for example, teaches physical science. She knows a lot about electricity. So, each year, she helps the newest and youngest members of the club build a potato battery. Students use nails, metal strips, copper wire, and potatoes to create currents, or flows of electrical energy. They use a machine called a voltmeter to measure the power of those currents. Potato batteries, I learned, don't make enough electricity to light a bulb or play my favorite music, but they're still fun to make.

Students can connect their potato battery to a voltmeter like this one to measure the strength of the electrical current.

The youngest Science Club members also do a volcano project. The goal is to make a model of a volcano that will erupt, or explode. Gooey lava is supposed to burst into the air and flow down the volcano's sides. It's a really fun activity.

There are different recipes for making a successful volcano. The ingredients are things people usually have in their kitchens. They include flour, salt, water, and oil. These help to make the "lava" thick and sticky. Red food coloring gives it the right color.

Vinegar and baking soda are the two most important ingredients for an explosion. When these combine, they create a lot of gas bubbles! A small amount of liquid dishwashing soap helps the other lava ingredients become foamy. The gassy, foamy mixture bursts up and out. The result is a "volcanic eruption" with "lava" running down the volcano's sides.

This year, we helped the younger students make their "lava." The recipe called for two tablespoons of baking soda for every 12 cups of lava. We made 18 cups of lava. How many tablespoons of baking soda did we use?

Rebound Ratios

Some older students in the club worked together this year on an activity called Rebound Ratios. A rebound happens when an object bounces back into the air after it hits a hard surface. For example, when we bounce a basketball, we push it toward the ground. The ball hits the floor and bounces back, or rebounds.

A rebound ratio describes the distance an object rebounds compared to the distance it was dropped. For example, let's say a basketball is dropped—not pushed—from a height of 200 centimeters. On one drop, it rebounds 166 centimeters. For this drop, this basketball has a rebound ratio of 200:166, or $\frac{200}{166}$.

To prepare for a possible mystery event at the Science Olympiad, we practiced finding rebound ratios in class. But we worked with small balls we could hold in one hand instead of basketballs.

To find the rebound ratio, we dropped a ball four times from the same height each time. Then, we calculated a **mean** rebound height for the drops. The mean is an average height. To find the mean, we added the rebound heights for each of the drops. Then, we divided the sum by the number of drops.

We dropped a tennis ball from a height of 150 centimeters each time. The rebound heights were 92, 91, 93.5, and 90.5 centimeters. What was the mean rebound height? What was the rebound ratio for this set of drops?

Next, we predicted the rebound height for the same tennis ball if we dropped it from a different height.

What height will the tennis ball rebound to if it is dropped a distance of 200 centimeters? This will have a proportional relationship to the rebound ratio calculated above. Round to the nearest whole number.

Bigger Than Real Life

In the Science Olympiad, students are given craft supplies and asked to build models of living things or parts of living things. We made models of lots of things in our club. One of our first activities was to make a model of a plant cell. **Cells** are the building blocks of all living things. Plants are made of cells. Animals are made of cells. Some living things are made of one cell. Others, such as humans, can have about 100 trillion cells.

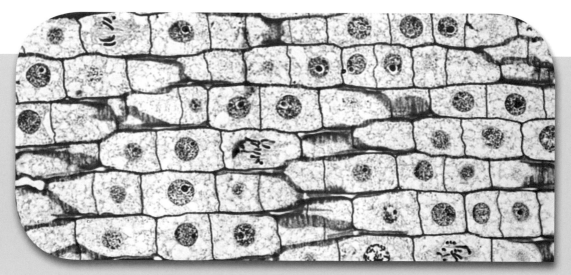

A microscope makes it possible to see cells, like these onion cells.

Most cells can be seen only with a **microscope**. A microscope is an instrument that has several lenses in it. Together, the lenses make objects look much larger than they really are. We often use microscopes in Science Club. In one activity, we looked at drops of pond water under a microscope.

It takes two minutes to prepare one slide. In all, our group spent 16 minutes preparing slides. How many slides did we prepare?

MATH AT WORK

An **architect** designs and draws the technical plans for buildings. In many cases, architects also supervise the actual construction of buildings.

Architects use their knowledge of math, physics, engineering, and building materials. They have to use all of this knowledge in order to design a building that will stay standing!

Artistic ability is also valuable to an architect. Most buildings are designed to be pleasing to the eye, as well as sturdy. So, architects make careful drawings. They also build three-dimensional models of their designs. The models are built to scale. That is, every measurement on the model is proportional to the corresponding measures on a finished building. This gives customers a detailed example of what a finished building will look like.

Build It

At the Science Olympiad, students in the upper grades do one or two work-at-school events. We are given the tasks ahead of time. We are encouraged to plant and grow something, or design and build something. Eventually, we take our project to the Olympiad to be tested and judged.

The Bust-a-Bridge Event is held each year. For this project, teams of four to six students design a bridge. The goal is to build a bridge to scale, using a given list of materials.

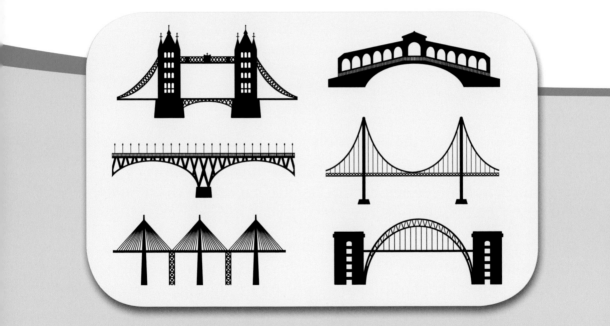

At the event, we want to be the last bridge standing—literally! The judges add weight to each bridge, a small amount at a time. They add the same weight to each bridge in the competition. They want to find out which team's bridge holds the largest load. The bridge that doesn't break wins the gold medal.

For the Bust-a-Bridge event, teams research different types of bridges, such as arch, suspension, and cable-wire bridges. Then, we are given a real-world bridge to model, and a scale to use for designing it.

One year, our school's team modeled a cable-wire bridge. They used a scale of 1:12 for the model. This meant that one unit of length in the model represented 12 units of length on the real bridge.

This year, teams modeled a stone arch bridge. For our model, we let 0.5 inches in the model represent 8 feet in the real bridge. The real stone arch bridge was 640 feet long and 20 feet wide.

What were the length and width of our model bridge?

The Float-a-Boat challenge is another yearly work-at-school event. It's similar to the Bust-a-Bridge event—you can guess what happens to the model boats at the Olympiad!

The Float-a-Boat event challenges us to understand how large, heavy boats can float. A ratio is the secret.

First, we have to understand **mass**. Mass is the amount of matter in an object or substance. A boat, for example, has mass. Next, we have to understand **volume**. Volume is the space a substance or an object takes up. A boat takes up space. So, it has volume.

Finally, we are ready to understand **density** as a ratio. Density describes how much matter is in a certain volume. So, we can say that it is the ratio of mass to volume. Density $= \frac{\text{mass}}{\text{volume}}$

We can write the density of pure water as: $\frac{1 \text{ g}}{\text{cm}^3}$. Matter with greater density than this sinks. Matter with less density floats.

For example, imagine dropping a cork into a bucket of water. The cork's density is $\frac{0.24 \text{ g}}{\text{cm}^3}$. Will the cork float or sink? Why?

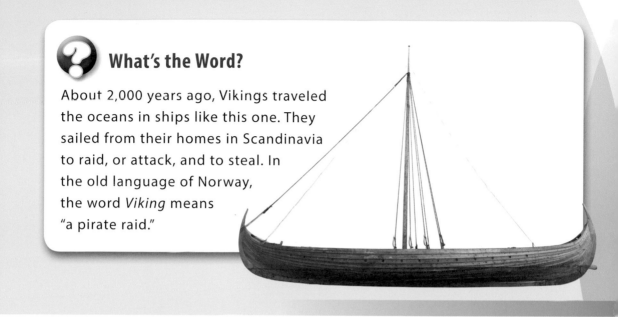

This year, our school's Float-a-Boat team had two goals. They wanted their model boat to have a mass of 1 kilogram. They also wanted it to be able to hold 30 kilograms without sinking. All together, then, their boat would have a total mass of 31 kilograms. But mass is only one part of the density ratio. Next, the team had to determine what volume their boat would need to have.

The team began by solving a ratio. They figured out what volume their boat needed to have to make the boat's density *equal* to the density of water. What was the boat's volume?

$$\frac{1,000 \text{ kg}}{\text{m}^3} = \frac{31 \text{ kg}}{?}$$

Once the team calculated this volume, they designed their model to have a *greater* volume. Increasing the boat's volume decreased its density. That was the trick to making the boat float. Its density would be less than the density of water. The team would successfully complete the float-a-boat challenge!

Modeling the JWST

The rules of the Science Olympiad allow students to display models without entering them into a specific contest. This year, a team made a model of the James Webb Space Telescope (JWST).

Scientists and engineers have been planning and building the JWST since 1996. Once in space, the JWST will circle the sun in the same path as Earth's orbit. In our club, we learned a lot about the telescope—what part of the **electromagnetic spectrum** it will view, how far away from Earth it will travel, and how big it is. The electromagnetic spectrum is the range of radiation, or energy, given off by the sun in the form of light, heat, x-rays, and particles.

Did You Know?

The James Webb Space Telescope is so big that it must be folded up in order to fit inside a launch rocket. Once the telescope is in space, it will unfold slowly, like a flower the size of a tennis court!

An artist's idea of the James Webb Space Telescope (JWST) in space

The JWST has several mirrors. Engineers and scientists designed the enormous main mirror to be made of smaller sections. The telescope itself will be shielded from the sun. The shield will be made of five layers of material. And it will be about the length of a tennis court.

The main mirror for the telescope has a **diameter**, or distance across, of 6.5 meters. Each of the 18 sections of the main mirror is shaped like a **hexagon**, or six-sided polygon. Each hexagon has a diameter of 1.32 meters.

For their JWST model, the team used a scale of 1:6, where 1 meter on the model represented 6 meters on the actual telescope.

What was the diameter of the main mirror on the model? What was the diameter of each hexagonal section on the model? Round each answer to the nearest hundredth of a meter.

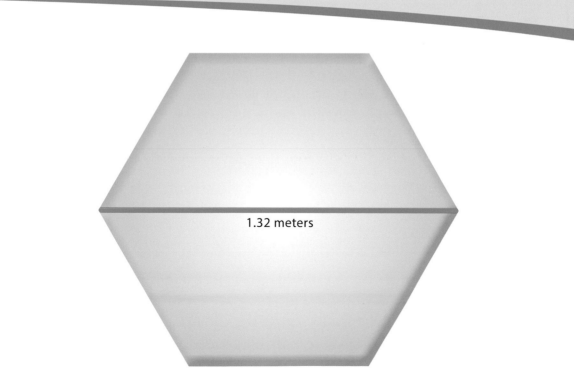

1.32 meters

Laser Lay-up

The Laser Lay-up is one of the Science Olympiad events that middle school students often get to do. We have to wear serious protective glasses, because we work with a laser beam! But it's a fun event to practice for and to participate in.

Judges at the Science Olympiad set up a laser and a target. Then they turn on the laser to show students the straight path between the laser and the target. Next, the judges cover the target. Students measure angles and set up two mirrors so they can bounce the light twice but still hit the target.

This is more difficult to do than it may sound. Students use flat mirrors and clay for holding the mirrors in place. They also have tools for measuring angles and string to model the light beam. Students have only three minutes to set up the mirrors. Judges measure how accurately the beam of light strikes the target.

Olympiad Volunteers

The Science Olympiad is organized entirely by volunteers. The volunteers include teachers from elementary, middle, and high schools. Teachers from the community college and university also help out. So do some professional scientists and engineers.

While students are busy with their work-at-school projects, volunteers get everything ready for the big event. They begin by finding a location that's large enough to hold all of the participants and projects.

Next, they make a schedule of events. They send out information to all the schools and keep track of the number of schools participating each year. They also select the events that will happen, and they make sure that all necessary equipment is on hand.

Science Olympiad volunteers plan the big day.

One popular event at the Science Olympiad that takes planning is another work-at-school project. Students design and build a hand-held water pump. At the Olympiad, they use their water pump to move water from a bucket into a large **graduated cylinder**. The team that fills the cylinder in the shortest time wins the event.

The volunteers organizing the event make sure graduated cylinders and buckets are on hand. Some of them also act as judges. They look for other volunteers to serve as judges, too.

The ratio of judges needed per number of teams participating in an event is 2:3. If an event has 33 teams participating, how many judges are needed for that event?

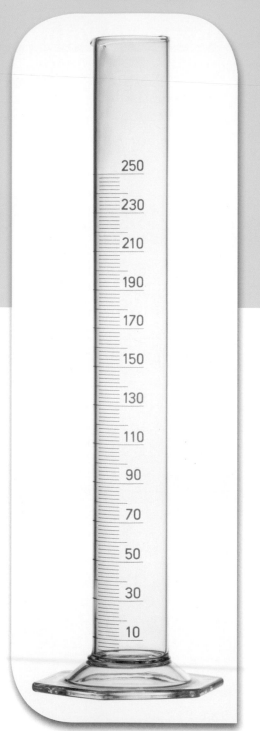

A graduated cylinder

This year, volunteers sent out information saying that there was a work-at-school event to build a working traffic light. They sent the rules and a list of materials students needed for the project. They also provided some of the electrical wiring after we told them how many teams would be participating. We planned to enter two teams. Each team made a traffic light with three lights: one red, one yellow, and one green.

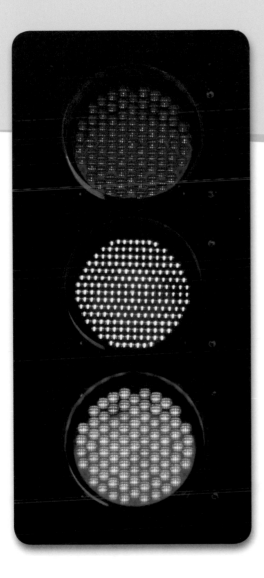

For every three lights used to make a traffic light, each team was given $1\frac{1}{2}$ feet of wire. What was the total length of wire our two teams received for the traffic light project?

In the days before the Science Olympiad, volunteers are extremely busy preparing materials for the student events. They make signs that help teams know where to go and where to set up. They print copies of the schedule. They work with teachers from the schools to know how many students are coming and what events they have prepared to participate in.

This year, the organizers needed chemistry teachers to prepare **solutions** for a chemistry event called Mystery Solutions. A solution is a mixture in which all of a substance is mixed evenly in a liquid, like water. In this event, high school chemistry students use lab equipment to test a set of unknown solutions. The goal is to identify as many solutions as possible in a set amount of time.

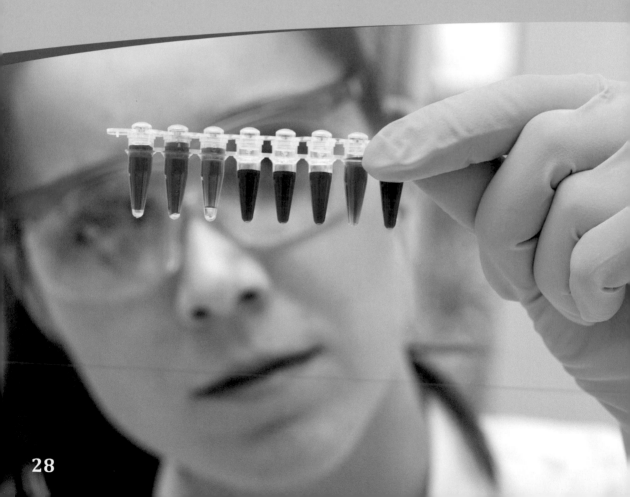

One of the chemicals students usually have to identify in Mystery Solutions is sodium iodide. Sodium iodide is sometimes added to table salt to give the human body the iodine it needs to remain healthy.

A chemist prepared the solutions the day before the Science Olympiad. She had to make enough samples for all of the teams participating in the event. One batch, or quantity, of the solution was enough to make four samples. Each team used one sample. There were 14 teams that planned to participate. How many batches did the chemist need to prepare?

To make one batch, the chemist must mix the chemical and water in a specific proportion. For the sodium iodide, she used 178.8 grams of sodium iodide per 100 milliliters of water. Recall the number of batches she needed to make for this year's event. How many grams of sodium iodide did she need to make this number of batches?

Finally, the big day arrives. Students meet with their teachers and teams. Younger students sit at large tables, where they work on mystery events. Older students set up their projects for demonstration and judging.

Observation is a very important part of the scientific process. In one mystery event, young students observe and describe items hidden inside black boxes. Students reach inside their boxes and feel the objects. Then, they describe their observations.

Newspaper Table is another event for the younger competitors. Students build tables using only three sheets of newspaper and tape. Their goal was to make the strongest table possible. The team whose table holds the greatest weight wins the event.

This shell once belonged to an animal called a cowrie, or a sea snail. There are more than 250 species of cowries.

Biologists are scientists who study living things. Some biologists study snails, animals that often live inside shells. Biologists measure the length and height of these shells. A shell's height is the length from the opening where the animal comes out to look for food and moves around to the highest point on the shell. Each species, or kind of snail, makes a shell with a certain ratio of length to height. So, ratios can help biologists identify snail species.

In one Olympiad biology event, students used ratios to identify snails. Then, they looked at a list of species, which included the length-to-height ratio for each species.

For example, one spotted shell had a length of seven centimeters, and its height was 3.5 centimeters. Students used a proportion to determine what kind of snail once lived in this spotted shell. Which species was it?

Species	Ratio of Length to Height (in cm)
A	2:1
B	3:2
C	4:1
D	1:1

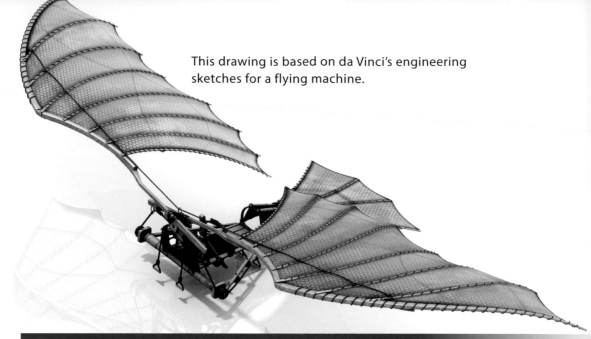

This drawing is based on da Vinci's engineering sketches for a flying machine.

CONNECTING TO HISTORY

Leonardo da Vinci was an Italian artist, scientist, and engineer who lived from 1452 to 1519. As an artist, he painted Mona Lisa, a woman wearing all black and smiling a mysterious smile. In addition to painting, Da Vinci also sculpted, played and created music, and sang.

As a scientist and engineer, Da Vinci was knowledgeable about many, many things! His areas of study included astronomy (the study of the stars), aeronautics (the study of flight), biology, cartography (map-making), chemistry, geography, geology (the study of Earth), and physics.

Da Vinci was an architect and engineer as well. He designed and invented many things. He also designed inventions that he never built, such as a flying machine, a helicopter, a parachute, and underwater diving gear.

This is a page from one of da Vinci's notebooks.

In 1502, da Vinci designed a bridge for a Turkish leader. But the leader thought the design was impossible to build.

Much of da Vinci's work, drawings, and ideas survived in a series of notebooks. About 8,000 pages of his notebooks survive today. These notebooks contain studies of the human body, scientific observations, and designs for engineering projects. An artist from Norway visited a museum where some of da Vinci's notebooks were displayed. He saw a sketch for the bridge da Vinci designed in 1502. The artist decided to build it.

In 2001, a ceremony was held to recognize the bridge in Aas, Norway. The bridge is the first engineering project based on da Vinci's sketches to ever be built.

Students at high schools and universities around the world are also building da Vinci's inventions. They use his sketches to build waterworks, engines, and even mechanical animals.

The Leaning Tower of Pisa stands in Pisa, Italy.

Throughout the day of the Science Olympiad, volunteers directed students to where they needed to be. Judges measured items and tested structures. Students answered questions, displayed finished projects, and built things out of various materials.

Some of the devices students built at home didn't work as planned. For example, a few of the hand-made water pumps broke. Judges and students got drenched. Boats that looked sturdy sunk under the smallest weights, while boats that appeared flimsy held more than 20 kilograms of cargo.

Some of the mystery events proved quite challenging. One event for middle school students was a building challenge. Each team was given a stack of building supplies and a picture of a tower. It was the Leaning Tower of Pisa in Pisa, Italy.

Students were given string, rubber bands, craft sticks, toothpicks, wooden coffee stirrers, rulers, scissors, file folders, cardboard, paper, newspaper, paper cups, and tennis balls. Students were allowed to use any and all of these supplies to build a model of the Leaning Tower of Pisa.

The materials came with a table of the tower's actual measurements. These included the different heights of the top of the tower. The goal was to choose a scale and then build a model in a set amount of time. Teams that built the most accurate model got more points.

Leaning Tower of Pisa

Dimensions	Measurement
Height on low side	55.86 meters
Height on high side	56.70 meters
Diameter at bottom of tower	15.48 meters

My team chose a ratio of 5:3. So, five centimeters on our model represented three meters on the actual tower. We rounded our calculations to the nearest hundredth. What were the three measurements on our model that were proportional to the measurements in the chart?

An event I really enjoyed was Dinosaur Parachutes! Olympiad volunteers gave each team a set of materials that included a small, plastic toy dinosaur, plastic garbage bags, a ruler, scissors, string, and a stopwatch.

In part one of the event, students found out how well parachutes of different sizes worked for the same toy dinosaur. Every parachute had to be square. In each trial, students used a different parachute and a stopwatch to measure how long it took the toy to reach the ground.

Students made the parachutes from garbage bags. They cut four strings for each parachute. Each piece of string was the same length, for all parachute sizes. They dropped the toy and parachute from the same height each time.

Each team collected data, or information, for how the different sizes of parachutes controlled the small dinosaur's fall. Then, we were given a bigger toy dinosaur. Students predicted what size parachutes were needed to let the bigger toy fall from the same height.

For example, one team started with a square parachute. Each side was 29 centimeters long. Their small dinosaur had a mass of 40 grams. They made a new parachute for a larger dinosaur toy with a mass of 65 grams. They used a proportion to determine how long to make each side of the new parachute. What was the length of each side of the new parachute? Round the answer to the nearest hundredth.

Many students get excited about robots! This year, teams designed robots in a work-to-school project. The robots had to be able to pop balloons.

Teams worked throughout the school year to design, build, program, and test their robots. At the Science Olympiad, teams compete to see whose robot can pop the most balloons in the shortest amount of time.

Building robots can be expensive, but there are ways to make it cheaper. Someone at our school donated a remote-controlled toy from home. The robot team used parts of this toy to make their robot, but they still needed some parts.

Mr. Mead found bags of extra parts at a local electronics store. The price was $7.00 for four bags. He bought 13 bags. How much did Mr. Mead pay for the bags?

One of the last events of the day for middle-school students was the Astronomy Triathlon. Astronomy is the study of objects in space, such as stars, planets, and galaxies. A triathlon is an event that has three parts.

Students studied astronomy all year in preparation for this event. At the Science Olympiad, they were given graph paper and tools for measuring distances and angles. Each team was asked to bring a simple calculator and pens or pencils.

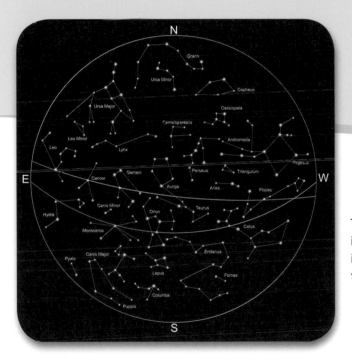

This constellation map identifies patterns of stars in the night sky. Are any of them familiar to you?

First, teams identified major stars, planets, and **constellations**, or groups of stars that seem to make patterns or pictures in the sky. Next, they were given data for a solar system other than ours. They had to figure out which planets in that system were likely to have water, be rocky like Earth, be gas giants like Jupiter, and so on. Finally, they used a scientific law to find out how far away some space objects are from Earth.

A Point of Light

Another astronomy challenge this year was to calculate the diameter of the sun. Science Olympiad volunteers sent a project description early in the year. It included a project design, a proportion, and a strong safety warning to never, never look directly at the sun.

The materials for the project included a notecard, a pin, and a ruler. Students used the pin to make a hole in the notecard. They let the sun shine through the pinhole onto a wall or piece of paper. This created an image of the sun. Then, they used a ruler to measure the diameter of the image and to measure the distance from the card to the image.

The project directions explained that the distance between the sun and Earth is 149,669,180 kilometers. Here is the proportion students were given:

$$\frac{\text{Diameter of Sun}}{\text{Distance between Sun and Earth}} = \frac{\text{Diameter of image of Sun}}{\text{Distance from pinhole to image}}$$

The team measured the distance from the pinhole in the note card to the sun's image on a wall. The distance was 31 centimeters. The diameter of the image was 0.29 centimeters.

Students used these measurements and a proportion to calculate the sun's diameter. What is the sun's diameter according to their calculations?

Finally, the Science Olympiad was over, but Mr. Mead challenged members of the Science Club to another project. We were still excited about our performance at the Science Olympiad. Teams in every age category had done really well. We even won a few medals! That excitement carried us into one last project for the year.

Plants rely on energy from the sun and chemicals in their cells to make food for growth and reproduction.

As a final chemistry activity for the year, we researched an **element**. An element is the simplest form of a substance that cannot be broken down into any other form. We chose the metal *manganese* for our research.

Manganese is used to color glass and to make iron tools stronger. And manganese is completely necessary to all life on Earth. Plant cells need it for photosynthesis, or to make their own food. And all cells need it to create energy.

Mr. Mead gave us a problem to solve, and offered to help. We started by finding the total mass of our club members. It is 841.8 kilograms. We estimated that the total amount of manganese in our bodies is 276 milligrams. The average weight of one student in Science Club is 36.6 kilograms.

About how much manganese is in each club member's body? How could we find the answer?

Idea 1: We could use a **tape diagram**. However, Mr. Mead thought it would be difficult to use tape diagrams with decimal numbers. He suggested that we think of a simpler method.

Idea 2: We could create a **table** of equivalent ratios. However, it would take too much time to build a table of multiples, Mr. Mead said.

Idea 3: We could find a **unit rate** to find the fourth term in a proportion. Mr. Mead thought that this method would work well, but we talked about one more idea before deciding.

Manganese crystals

We set up the proportion. Then, we found the unit rate.

$$\frac{276 \text{ mg}}{841.8 \text{ kg}} = \frac{? \text{ mg}}{36.6 \text{ kg}}$$

We found the unit rate by dividing the total number of milligrams in all club members by the total mass of all club members. Then, we multiplied the unit rate, or per kilogram rate, by the average mass of a club member.

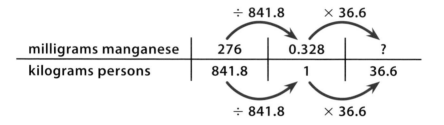

	÷ 841.8	× 36.6	
milligrams manganese	276	0.328	?
kilograms persons	841.8	1	36.6
	÷ 841.8	× 36.6	

About how much manganese is in each club member?

I was impressed to learn that my body has this much manganese in it! In fact, I was amazed by many things I learned this year for the Science Olympiad, and I'm excited to do it again next year.

Crystals of manganese and other minerals turned this wood into stone, or petrified wood.

WHAT COMES NEXT?

Work with an adult or with friends who would enjoy the challenge of building a bridge. There are many kinds of bridges, from ancient stone bridges to modern constructions, such as suspension bridges. Research the different kinds of bridges. Select one that appeals to you. Then, contact experts or use the Internet to find an example of this type of bridge in the real world. Find out as much as you can about its measurements, such as how long, tall, and wide it is. Then, use the following guidelines to build a model of the bridge.

Make a model bridge that is proportional to the real bridge. Choose a scale that works for you. Use only craft sticks and glue to create your model. You may want to test the strength of your bridge. Share your work with others. Encourage them to build a bridge, too. You can be the lead engineer on the project!

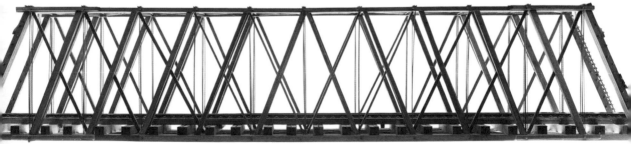

This is a wooden model of a truss bridge.

GLOSSARY

architect: a person who designs structures, such as buildings.

biologist(s): scientists who study living things.

cells: the basic unit or building block of all living things.

constellation(s): arrangements of stars in the sky that seem to form a picture.

corresponding: being in the same position or having the same measure.

density: a property of an object that describes its mass compared to its volume.

diameter: the distance from one side of a circle or polygon to the opposite side through the middle of the shape.

electromagnetic spectrum: the entire range of energy given off by stars as light and heat.

element: matter that is made up entirely of only one kind of atom.

equivalent: having the same value.

graduated cylinder: a tool used to measure a volume of liquid.

hexagon: a polygon with six sides.

mass: the amount of matter in a substance or object.

mean: the average value of a data set, found by dividing the sum of the addends, or numbers, in the set by the total number of addends; an average.

microscope: a tool that uses lenses to make objects look larger than they really are.

polygon: a closed, flat shape with at least three sides and in which all sides are straight lines.

proportion: a mathematical statement showing that two ratios are equivalent.

quadrilateral: a polygon with four sides.

ratio: a comparison of two numbers or measures using the operation of division.

scale: the ratio of length used in a drawing, map, or model to its length in reality.

similar: describes figures that have the same shape but are different sizes.

solution (chemistry): a mixture in which one substance is mixed evenly in a liquid, usually water.

table: a chart for organizing numbers, or data, to make them easier to find and compare.

tape diagram: a model that looks like a strip of tape used to show relationships between numbers.

terms: the parts of a proportion.

unit rate: a ratio of a dollar amount to a unit amount, such as cost per ounce of cereal.

volume: the amount of space a substance or object takes up, measured in cubic units.

FURTHER READING

FICTION
Steel Trapp: The Challenge, by Ridley Peterson, Disney Additions, 2008
Mac Slater vs. the City, by Tristan Bancks, Simon & Schuster Books for Young
    Readers, 2011

NONFICTION
Pythagoras and the Ratios: A Math Adventure, by Julie Ellis, Charlesbridge
    Publishing, 2010
Amazing Leonardo da Vinci Inventions You Can Build Yourself, by Maxine Anderson,
    Nomad Press, 2006

ADDITIONAL NOTES

The page references below provide answers to questions asked
throughout the book. Questions whose answers will vary are not addressed.

Page 13: 3 tablespoons

Page 15: mean rebound
height—91.75 cm;
rebound ratio—$\frac{150}{91.75}$; rebound
height—122 cm

Page 16: 8 slides

Page 19: The length is 40 inches.
The width is 1.25 inches.

Page 20: The cork will float because
it has less density than water.

Page 21: 0.03 m^3, or 31,000 cm^3

Page 23: 1.08 meters; 0.22 meter

Page 26: 22 judges

Page 27: 3 feet

Page 29: $3\frac{1}{2}$ (3.5) batches; 625.8 g

Page 31: Species A

Page 35: Height on low side—93.1
cm; Height on high side—94.5
cm; Diameter at bottom of
tower—25.8 cm

Page 37: 47.13 centimeters

Page 38: $22.75

Page 41: 1,400,131 km

Page 44: 12 mg

INDEX

CONTENT CONSULTANT

David T. Hughes

David is an experienced mathematics teacher, writer, presenter, and adviser. He serves as a consultant for the Partnership for Assessment of Readiness for College and Careers. David has also worked as the Senior Program Coordinator for the Charles A. Dana Center at The University of Texas at Austin and was an editor and contributor for the *Mathematics Standards in the Classroom* series.